BUSINESS COMMUNICATION

DR. ABHISHEK VENKTESHWAR

Dedicated to Acharya Institute of Technology

Contents

About The Author

About the Author:

Dr. Abhishek Venkteshwar
D.Lit.,PhD,PGCL(UK),M.Phil, PGDUT(AUS) ,KSET,Al DoE,MBA,
B.SC(UK)
Associate Professor, HOD-MBA and Director-Online MBA
Acharya Institute of Technology

Dr. Abhishek Venkteshwar has established a distinguished career in the field of education, spanning over a decade. He has held significant roles, notably as Assistant Director, UG Program Lead, and Assistant Professor at Alliance University, as well as Assistant Professor and Head of Department – Program Development and Student Affairs at Jain University. Additionally, he has served at Christ University and Amazon. Dr. Abhishek's expertise is particularly evident in his adept management of spectator engagement, highlighted by his pivotal role in orchestrating spectator experiences during the National level Khelo India University Games 2022, demonstrating a rare combination of academic excellence and organizational proficiency.

Dr. Abhishek's educational background is impressive, including a Postgraduate Certificate from the renowned London School of Business Administration, UK, and an honorary Doctor of Letters from the University of New Jerusalem. He holds a Ph.D., M.Phil., and MBA from Jain University, a Postgraduate Diploma in University Teaching from the University of Newcastle, Australia, and a B.Sc. (Honors) from Aston University. Notably, he completed the Motivation Pathways program with Toastmasters International, USA, showcasing his commitment to enhancing communication skills. His scholarly achievements include three gold medals for academic excellence and certification as an awarder by The Duke of Edinburgh Awards, UK. Dr. Abhishek's dedication to continuous learning is evident through certifications from prestigious institutions such as Harvard University, Yale University, IIM-Bengaluru, and ISB Hyderabad. He has published over 70 papers in esteemed UGC CARE/Scopus indexed international journals and authored over 25 textbooks across various management disciplines. Additionally, he serves as a Reviewer for the Asia Pacific Management Review at Elsevier and has appeared as a panelist on reputable television channels such as Republic and News 9.

Dr. Abhishek has received widespread recognition for his contributions, including the "Best Professor" award from RULA International Awards, Global Leadership Awards, and DR Research Awards in 2020. He has subsequently been honored with prestigious awards such as the Global Best Teacher Award, Vidya Bhushan Award for Best Teacher, Asian Conclave Best Professor, and Wall of Fame Best Educationist Award. His teaching philosophy revolves around the 3 E Approach - Education, Engagement, and Entertainment, emphasizing the importance of engagement in facilitating effective learning. His innovative pedagogy, "Game of Cases," integrates traditional teaching methods with interactive learning experiences, reflecting his dedication to creating dynamic educational environments.

Foreword

The book delves deeper into the dynamics of intra-organizational and B2B/B2C communication, shedding light on power dynamics, decision-making processes, and ethical considerations. With a focus on interpersonal communication theories and applications, readers are equipped with the tools necessary to navigate complex organizational structures and foster productive relationships. Moving forward, advanced topics such as the Coordinated Management of Meaning and Fisher's Model in Communication provide readers with a sophisticated understanding of communication dynamics.

Dr. Chandni Patak
Professor, Alliance University

Preface

In "Mastering Business Communication: Strategies for Success," readers are taken on an immersive journey through the intricate landscape of modern business communication. The book begins by laying a solid foundation with an exploration of the fundamental principles of business communication, encompassing both verbal and nonverbal aspects, along with an examination of key theories and strategies. Through insightful discussions on overcoming communication barriers, readers gain valuable insights into identifying and addressing obstacles that hinder effective communication within organizations.

Additionally, the book offers practical guidance on project and research report writing, oral communication, and marketing strategies. From crafting impactful emails to delivering persuasive presentations, readers learn the art of effective communication in various contexts. Furthermore, insights into crisis communication and brand management empower readers to navigate challenging situations with confidence and finesse. With additional resources provided for further exploration, "Mastering Business Communication" serves as an indispensable resource for MBA students and professionals alike, offering comprehensive coverage of essential communication strategies for success in today's Business landscape.

Acknowledgements

This book represents a significant milestone in my academic journey, and I am deeply grateful for the steadfast support we have received. My heartfelt appreciation goes to B. Premnath Reddy, the Founder Chairman of Acharya Institutes; Mr. Krishna Basani, Managing Director; Dr. Rajath Hegde M.M., Principal, Acharya Institute of Technology; Prof. C.K. Marigowda, Vice Principal; and Dr. Rajeshwari, Dean-Academics. I also want to acknowledge the pivotal roles played by my esteemed colleagues in the Department of MBA: Dr. Juin, Dr. Nijaguna, Dr. Renuka, Dr. Raina, Dr. Monica, Dr. Mahak, Prof. Archana, Prof. Suhas, Prof. Bhavya, Prof. Channakeshava, Prof. Anithabai, Prof. Netravati, Prof. Harshitha, Prof. Kirthika, Prof. Harshini, Prof. Rohith, Prof. Yogesh, Prof. Dhanalakshmi, Prof. Nikiha, Prof. Anju, Prof. Pasha, Prof. Sabita, Prof. Sajita, and Ms. Savitha, for their invaluable contributions to the realization of this endeavor.

I must thank my mother, Meenakshi, who has stood by me through thick and thin. My late father, Venkteshwar, and my grandparents, Ms. Indira Shanmugam, Ms. Shymala Vinayakam, and Mr. Shanmugam, have been my constant source of inspiration. My aunts, Nirupa and Deepa, and my confidant, Ms. Geeta Samant, have steadfastly supported me throughout my journey. My colleague, friend, and inspiration, Dr. Kiran Maney, has profoundly influenced my professional journey.

Additionally, I extend heartfelt appreciation to all members of our group, whose collaboration and dedication have been integral to the completion of this work. Each individual's contribution has been invaluable, and I am truly appreciative of the collective effort in this academic pursuit.

CHAPTER ONE

INTRODUCTION TO BUSINESS COMMUNICATION

Definition and Importance of Business Communication

Business communication is the process of exchanging information within an organization, between different organizations, or with external stakeholders to facilitate business activities. It encompasses various forms of communication, including verbal, written, and nonverbal interactions. Effective business communication is essential for the smooth functioning of an organization, as it facilitates decision-making, problem-solving, coordination, and collaboration. Moreover, it plays a crucial role in achieving organizational goals, maintaining relationships with customers and stakeholders, and enhancing overall performance.

Verbal and Nonverbal Communication

Verbal communication involves the use of spoken or written words to convey messages. It includes face-to-face conversations, telephone calls, presentations, meetings, and written documents such as emails, memos, reports, and letters. On the other hand, nonverbal communication encompasses the use of body language, facial expressions, gestures, posture, tone of voice, eye contact, and other nonverbal cues to convey messages. Nonverbal communication often complements verbal messages and can significantly impact how messages are interpreted and understood.

Basic Theories of Communication

Several theoretical models explain the process of communication and how messages are transmitted and received:

- **Shannon-Weaver Model**: This linear model conceptualizes communication as a process involving a sender who encodes a message, which is transmitted through a channel to a receiver who decodes the message. Feedback completes the communication loop.
- **Berlo's Model**: Emphasizing the importance of the sender, message, channel, receiver, and feedback, this model highlights the dynamic nature of communication and the need for effective encoding and decoding of messages.
- **Transactional Model**: Unlike linear models, the transactional model views communication as a simultaneous exchange of messages between sender and receiver. It considers the influence of context, environment, and feedback on the communication process, emphasizing the bidirectional nature of communication.

Nonverbal Communication

Nonverbal communication plays a significant role in conveying emotions, attitudes, and intentions. It includes facial expressions, body language, gestures, posture, proxemics (use of personal space), paralinguistics (tone of voice, pitch, volume), and other nonverbal cues. Nonverbal cues often provide additional context to verbal messages and can influence how messages are perceived and interpreted by receivers.

Barriers to Communication and Overcoming Strategies

Despite its importance, effective communication can be hindered by various barriers:

- **Language Barriers**: Differences in language proficiency or language used can lead to misunderstandings. Overcoming language barriers may involve providing language training, using interpreters or translators, and simplifying language.
- **Cultural Differences**: Varied cultural norms, values, and communication styles can create barriers to understanding. Strategies to overcome cultural differences include cultural sensitivity training, respecting cultural diversity, and fostering cross-cultural communication.
- **Psychological Barriers**: Personal emotions, attitudes, and perceptions can influence communication effectiveness. Overcoming psychological barriers may require creating a supportive and inclusive work environment, encouraging open communication, and addressing

individual concerns.

- **Physical Barriers**: Environmental factors such as noise, distance, and technological limitations can impede communication. Strategies to overcome physical barriers include using appropriate communication tools and technology, minimizing noise and distractions, and arranging face-to-face communication when possible.
- **Semantic Barriers**: Differences in interpretation and understanding of words, symbols, or meanings can lead to communication breakdowns. Overcoming semantic barriers involves clarifying meanings, using simple and clear language, and encouraging feedback and clarification.

Effective business communication is essential for organizational success, as it facilitates collaboration, decision-making, problem-solving, and relationship-building. By understanding the various forms of communication, basic theories, and strategies to overcome barriers, organizations can enhance communication effectiveness and achieve their goals. Continuous evaluation and refinement of communication practices are necessary to adapt to changing needs and environments in today's dynamic business landscape.

Case Study: Overcoming Communication Challenges in a Multinational Corporation

Background:

XYZ Corporation is a multinational company operating in various countries with diverse cultures, languages, and communication norms. The company specializes in manufacturing and distributing consumer electronics products globally. Despite its success in the market, XYZ Corporation faces communication challenges that hinder its efficiency and effectiveness.

Scenario:

XYZ Corporation recently launched a new product line aimed at capturing emerging markets in Asia, including China, India, and Japan. However, during the initial phase of product development and market entry, the company encountered several communication challenges:

Language Barriers: The project team comprised members from different countries, each with varying levels of proficiency in English, the primary language of communication within the company. Language barriers resulted in misunderstandings, misinterpretations, and delays in decision-making.

Cultural Differences: Team members from different cultural backgrounds had diverse communication styles, preferences, and norms. These differences led to conflicts, lack of cohesion, and difficulties in building rapport and trust among team members.

Technological Limitations: The use of outdated communication tools and technologies hindered effective collaboration and information sharing among team members spread across different time zones. Technical glitches, connectivity issues, and compatibility problems further exacerbated communication challenges.

Barriers to Innovation: Due to communication barriers, valuable ideas, insights, and feedback from team members were often overlooked or dismissed, hindering innovation and creativity in product development and marketing strategies.

Strategies for Overcoming Communication Challenges:

Language Training: XYZ Corporation invested in language training programs to improve the English proficiency of team members and provided language support services, such as translation and interpretation, to facilitate communication.

Cultural Sensitivity Training: The company organized cultural sensitivity training sessions to raise awareness about cultural differences and promote understanding, respect, and appreciation for diverse perspectives and communication styles.

Technology Upgrade: XYZ Corporation upgraded its communication infrastructure by implementing modern communication tools and technologies, such as video conferencing, collaboration platforms, and project management software, to enhance virtual collaboration and information sharing.

Cross-Functional Teams: The company formed cross-functional teams comprising members from different departments and regions to foster collaboration, diversity of thought, and collective problem-solving.

Feedback Mechanisms: XYZ Corporation implemented feedback mechanisms, such as regular meetings, surveys, and suggestion boxes, to encourage open communication, address concerns, and gather input from team members.

Results:

By implementing these strategies, XYZ Corporation successfully overcame communication challenges and achieved the following outcomes:

- Improved collaboration and teamwork among diverse team members
- Enhanced decision-making and problem-solving processes
- Increased innovation and creativity in product development and marketing strategies
- Strengthened relationships and trust among team members
- Streamlined communication processes and reduced misunderstandings and conflicts.

Conclusion:

Effective communication is critical for multinational corporations like XYZ Corporation to succeed in today's globalized business environment. By recognizing and addressing communication challenges proactively through language training, cultural sensitivity, technological upgrades, and collaborative strategies, organizations can overcome barriers and unlock the full potential of their teams to achieve their goals and objectives.

CHAPTER TWO

Intra-organizational and B2B/B2C Communication

Power Dynamics in Organizations:

- **Definition:** Power dynamics refer to the distribution and utilization of power among individuals and groups within an organization.
- **Hierarchy and Authority:** Organizational structures often establish hierarchies where power is concentrated at the top levels, influencing decision-making processes and communication flows.
- **Influence and Control:** Power dynamics also involve the ability to influence others' behavior and control resources, which can impact communication interactions and relationships.

Decision Making Processes:

- **Rational Decision Making:** This model involves a systematic approach to decision-making, where individuals gather information, evaluate alternatives, and choose the most suitable course of action based on rational analysis.
- **Bounded Rationality:** In practice, decision-makers often face limitations in processing information and evaluating all possible alternatives, leading to bounded rationality where decisions are made based on satisficing rather than optimizing.
- **Intuitive Decision Making:** Sometimes decisions are made intuitively, relying on gut feelings, past experiences, and unconscious processes

rather than deliberate analysis.

Motivation Techniques:

- **Goal Setting:** Establishing clear and challenging goals motivates employees by providing a sense of direction and purpose.
- **Rewards and Recognition:** Offering rewards, such as bonuses or promotions, and recognizing employees' achievements reinforces desired behaviors and encourages high performance.
- **Empowerment:** Giving employees autonomy and decision-making authority fosters a sense of ownership and responsibility, motivating them to take initiative and contribute to organizational goals.
- **Feedback:** Providing regular feedback on performance helps employees understand their strengths and areas for improvement, increasing their motivation to excel.

Ethical Considerations in Business Communication:

- **Honesty and Integrity:** Ethical communication requires honesty and transparency in conveying information and representing the organization's interests.
- **Respect for Stakeholders:** Organizations should respect the rights and interests of stakeholders, including employees, customers, and the community, in their communication practices.
- **Fairness and Equity:** Ethical communication entails treating all stakeholders fairly and equitably, avoiding discrimination, favoritism, or manipulation.
- **Compliance with Laws and Regulations:** Businesses must adhere to legal and regulatory requirements governing communication, such as truth in advertising laws and data privacy regulations.

Interpersonal Communication Theories and Applications:

- **Social Penetration Theory:**

  - Developed by Altman and Taylor, this theory posits that relationships develop through self-disclosure, gradually revealing deeper layers of one's personality and emotions.

- As individuals share more personal information, relationships progress from superficial levels to deeper levels of intimacy, fostering trust and connection.

- **Uncertainty Reduction Theory:**

  - Berger and Calabrese proposed this theory, which suggests that individuals seek to reduce uncertainty in initial interactions with others.
  - Strategies such as seeking information, asking questions, and engaging in communication help reduce uncertainty and increase predictability, leading to more positive attitudes and relational satisfaction.

- **Relational Dialectics Theory:**

  - Baxter and Montgomery introduced this theory, which explores the tensions and contradictions inherent in interpersonal relationships.
  - Relationships are characterized by dialectical tensions, such as autonomy/connection and openness/closedness, which individuals must navigate and negotiate to maintain relational harmony and satisfaction.

Case Study: Improving Communication in a Manufacturing Company

Background: ABC Manufacturing Company is a leading manufacturer of automotive parts with operations spanning multiple locations globally. Despite its success in the industry, ABC Manufacturing Company faces communication challenges that affect its operational efficiency and employee morale.

Scenario: ABC Manufacturing Company encounters the following communication issues:

Power Dynamics: Hierarchical structures within the organization create power imbalances and hinder effective communication between management and frontline employees. Employees may feel intimidated or reluctant to voice their opinions or concerns, leading to disengagement and decreased productivity.

Decision Making Processes: Decision-making processes are centralized, with limited input from employees at lower levels of the organization. Lack of participation and involvement in decision-making leads to feelings of disempowerment and alienation among employees.

Motivation: Employees lack motivation due to limited opportunities for recognition, growth, and development. The absence of clear communication regarding performance expectations and goals contributes to employee demotivation and disengagement.

Ethical Concerns: Instances of unethical behavior, such as favoritism, nepotism, and lack of transparency, erode trust and credibility within the organization. Ethical lapses in communication undermine employee morale and organizational reputation.

Strategies for Improvement:

1. **Empowerment:** Implement decentralized decision-making processes to empower employees and encourage participation in decision-making. Create avenues for employee input, feedback, and suggestions to foster a sense of ownership and accountability.

2. **Communication Training:** Provide communication training programs for employees at all levels to enhance their communication skills and confidence. Offer workshops on active listening, conflict resolution, and assertive communication to promote effective interpersonal interactions.

3. **Recognition and Rewards:** Establish recognition and rewards programs to acknowledge employee contributions and achievements. Communicate clear performance expectations and provide regular feedback to motivate employees and foster a culture of appreciation.

4. **Ethical Guidelines:** Develop and communicate clear ethical guidelines and standards of conduct to guide employee behavior. Encourage openness, honesty, and integrity in all communication processes, and address ethical concerns promptly and transparently.

5. **Feedback Mechanisms:** Implement formal feedback mechanisms, such as employee surveys, suggestion boxes, and performance evaluations, to solicit employee feedback and address concerns. Create a culture of open communication where employees feel valued and heard.

Expected Outcomes: By implementing these strategies, ABC Manufacturing Company aims to achieve the following outcomes:

- Improved employee engagement, morale, and satisfaction

- Enhanced communication effectiveness and transparency
- Increased collaboration and innovation within the organization
- Strengthened ethical culture and organizational integrity
- Greater productivity, efficiency, and competitiveness in the market

CHAPTER THREE

ADVANCED ORGANIZATIONAL COMMUNICATION

Coordinated Management of Meaning:

- **Definition:** Coordinated Management of Meaning (CMM) is a communication theory developed by W. Barnett Pearce and Vernon Cronen. It focuses on how individuals create and interpret meaning through communication and how these meanings shape their interactions and relationships.
- **Key Concepts:**

  - **Coordination:** CMM emphasizes the importance of coordinating actions and interpretations within social contexts to create shared meanings.
  - **Hierarchical Structures:** The theory explores how communication patterns reflect hierarchical structures of power and authority within organizations.
  - **Cultural Context:** Cultural norms, values, and beliefs influence the coordination of meaning in communication interactions.

- **Applications:** CMM provides insights into how organizations can improve communication effectiveness by promoting shared understanding, managing conflicts, and fostering collaboration among employees.

Dramatism Theory and Applications:

- **Definition:** Dramatism theory, developed by Kenneth Burke, views human interaction as a form of drama, with individuals as actors who use language and symbols to create narratives and enact roles.
- **Key Concepts:**

  - **The Pentad:** Burke's dramatistic pentad consists of five elements—act, scene, agent, agency, and purpose—that shape the rhetorical analysis of communication.
  - **Identification and Division:** Dramatism examines how individuals seek identification with others and use division to differentiate themselves from others in communication.

- **Applications:** Dramatism theory offers insights into organizational rhetoric, conflict resolution, and leadership communication strategies.

Fisher's Model in Communication:

- **Definition:** Fisher's narrative paradigm, proposed by Walter Fisher, suggests that humans are inherently storytellers who use narratives to make sense of their experiences and persuade others.
- **Key Concepts:**

  - **Narrative Rationality:** Fisher argues that individuals judge the credibility of narratives based on coherence (internal consistency) and fidelity (relation to shared beliefs and values).
  - **Narrative Probability:** The theory posits that individuals assess the likelihood of a narrative based on its narrative probability (plausibility) and narrative fidelity (truthfulness).

- **Applications:** Fisher's model informs organizational communication practices by emphasizing the persuasive power of storytelling and the importance of crafting compelling narratives that resonate with audiences.

Johari Window and its Impact on Communication:

- **Definition:** The Johari Window, developed by Joseph Luft and Harrington Ingham, is a communication model that represents the relationships between self-disclosure and feedback in interpersonal interactions.
- **Key Concepts:**

  - **Four Quadrants:** The Johari Window consists of four quadrants—open, blind, hidden, and unknown—that represent different aspects of self-awareness and mutual understanding.
  - **Self-Disclosure:** The model illustrates how self-disclosure can increase the open area (known to self and others) and reduce the blind area (known to others but not to self) through feedback and reflection.

- **Applications:** The Johari Window is used in organizational settings to promote self-awareness, build trust, and enhance interpersonal relationships through increased transparency and feedback.

AIDA Model in Marketing Communication:

- **Definition:** The AIDA model, an acronym for Attention, Interest, Desire, and Action, is a framework used in marketing and advertising to guide the creation of persuasive communication messages.
- **Key Concepts:**

  - **Attention:** Grabbing the audience's attention through compelling headlines, visuals, or opening statements.
  - **Interest:** Generating interest by highlighting the benefits and unique selling points of the product or service.
  - **Desire:** Creating desire or need for the product by appealing to emotions and addressing consumer aspirations or pain points.
  - **Action:** Prompting the audience to take action, such as making a purchase, signing up for a newsletter, or visiting a website.

- **Applications:** The AIDA model informs marketing communication strategies by outlining the sequential steps needed to guide consumers from awareness to action, ultimately driving sales and achieving marketing objectives.

Case Study: Enhancing Organizational Communication at XYZ Corporation

Background: XYZ Corporation, a multinational technology company, is experiencing communication challenges that impact productivity and employee morale. Despite having a diverse workforce and innovative products, ineffective communication practices hinder collaboration and hinder organizational performance.

Scenario: XYZ Corporation faces the following communication issues:

Cross-Cultural Communication: With employees from diverse cultural backgrounds, communication barriers arise due to differences in language, communication styles, and cultural norms. Misunderstandings and conflicts often occur, leading to decreased collaboration and efficiency.

Leadership Communication: Communication from top management lacks transparency and clarity, leading to confusion and ambiguity among employees. Lack of direction and inconsistent messaging from leaders result in decreased morale and motivation.

Information Overload: Employees are overwhelmed with excessive information from various communication channels, including emails, meetings, and digital platforms. This information overload leads to cognitive overload, decreased attention span, and difficulty prioritizing tasks.

Feedback Mechanisms: The organization lacks effective feedback mechanisms for employees to voice their opinions, provide suggestions, and address concerns. Employees feel unheard and undervalued, leading to disengagement and decreased commitment to organizational goals.

Strategies for Improvement:

1. **Cross-Cultural Training:** Implement cross-cultural training programs to enhance employees' cultural competence and communication skills. Provide resources and support for language learning and cultural awareness to facilitate effective communication across diverse teams.
2. **Transparent Communication:** Promote transparency and openness in leadership communication by providing regular updates, clarifying expectations, and soliciting feedback from employees. Establish clear communication channels for sharing organizational goals, strategies, and performance metrics.
3. **Information Management:** Streamline communication channels and prioritize information to reduce information overload. Implement

communication guidelines and protocols to ensure relevant and timely information dissemination while minimizing redundant messages.

4. **Feedback Culture:** Foster a feedback culture where employees feel comfortable providing feedback and raising concerns. Establish formal and informal feedback mechanisms, such as surveys, suggestion boxes, and regular one-on-one meetings, to encourage open communication and address employee needs.

Expected Outcomes: By implementing these strategies, XYZ Corporation aims to achieve the following outcomes:

- Improved cross-cultural communication and collaboration among diverse teams
- Increased transparency and clarity in leadership communication, fostering trust and engagement
- Enhanced information management practices, reducing information overload and improving productivity
- Cultivation of a feedback culture that empowers employees to voice their opinions and contribute to organizational success

CHAPTER FOUR

Project and Research Report Writing

Writing Effective Emails and Conveying Negative Messages:

- **Effective Email Communication:**

  - Clarity and Conciseness: Emails should be clear, concise, and to the point to ensure the recipient understands the message.
  - Professional Tone: Maintain a professional tone and use appropriate language and etiquette in all email communications.
  - Subject Line: Use a clear and descriptive subject line to summarize the purpose of the email and grab the recipient's attention.
  - Structure: Organize emails with a clear introduction, body, and conclusion, and use bullet points or numbered lists for readability.

- **Conveying Negative Messages:**

  - Empathy and Sensitivity: Approach negative messages with empathy and sensitivity, considering the recipient's feelings and perspective.
  - Directness: Be direct and straightforward in conveying negative news, avoiding ambiguity or mixed messages.
  - Offer Solutions: Provide solutions or alternatives to mitigate the impact of the negative message and demonstrate a commitment to resolving issues.

- Follow-Up: Offer opportunities for further discussion or clarification and be available to address any concerns or questions the recipient may have.

Report Writing Techniques:

- **Purpose and Audience:** Identify the purpose of the report and the intended audience to tailor the content and tone accordingly.
- **Structure:** Organize the report with a clear structure, including sections such as an executive summary, introduction, methodology, findings, conclusions, and recommendations.
- **Clarity and Precision:** Use clear and precise language to convey information, avoiding jargon or unnecessary technical terms that may confuse readers.
- **Visual Aids:** InBusiness visual aids such as tables, charts, and graphs to present data and information in a visually appealing and accessible format.
- **Citation and Referencing:** Properly cite sources and provide references to support assertions and findings, following a recognized citation style such as APA or MLA.

Writing Agendas and Minutes of Meetings:

- **Agendas:**

  - Agenda Purpose: Clearly outline the purpose and objectives of the meeting to inform participants of the topics to be discussed and the expected outcomes.
  - Time Allocation: Allocate sufficient time for each agenda item and prioritize topics based on importance and urgency.
  - Distribution: Distribute the agenda to all meeting participants in advance to allow adequate preparation and participation.

- **Minutes:**

  - Record Keeping: Take detailed notes during the meeting to accurately capture discussions, decisions, and action points.

- Format: Organize minutes in a structured format, including key discussion points, decisions made, and action items assigned.
- Distribution: Distribute minutes to all meeting participants promptly after the meeting to ensure accountability and follow-up on action items.

Research Report Writing Guidelines:

- **Research Objectives:** Clearly define the research objectives and research questions to guide the report's scope and focus.
- **Literature Review:** Conduct a thorough literature review to provide context, background information, and theoretical framework for the research.
- **Methodology:** Describe the research methodology, including data collection methods, sample selection, and data analysis techniques, to ensure transparency and replicability.
- **Findings and Analysis:** Present the research findings and analysis in a logical and systematic manner, using tables, charts, and graphs to enhance clarity and interpretation.
- **Conclusion and Recommendations:** Summarize the key findings and conclusions of the research and provide actionable recommendations for future research or practical applications.

Brainstorming Techniques for Project Development:

- **Free Association:** Encourage participants to freely associate ideas without judgment or criticism, allowing creativity to flow and generate innovative solutions.
- **Mind Mapping:** Use visual brainstorming techniques such as mind mapping to visually organize ideas and explore connections between different concepts.
- **Round-Robin Brainstorming:** Facilitate a structured brainstorming session where each participant contributes one idea in turn, ensuring equal participation and diversity of perspectives.
- **SWOT Analysis:** Conduct a SWOT (Strengths, Weaknesses, Opportunities, Threats) analysis to systematically evaluate the project's internal and external factors and identify potential areas for improvement and growth.

Case Study: Improving Project Communication at ABC Corporation

Background: ABC Corporation, a construction company, is facing challenges in project communication that affect project coordination and efficiency. Despite having skilled teams and resources, communication gaps lead to delays, misunderstandings, and cost overruns.

Scenario: ABC Corporation encounters the following communication issues:

Communication Breakdowns: Poor communication between project teams, subcontractors, and stakeholders leads to misunderstandings, delays in decision-making, and conflicts.

Lack of Clarity: Project requirements, timelines, and expectations are not clearly communicated, resulting in confusion and misalignment among team members.

Ineffective Reporting: Project reports are inconsistent, incomplete, or delayed, making it difficult for stakeholders to track progress and make informed decisions.

Unclear Roles and Responsibilities: Unclear roles and responsibilities contribute to overlaps, gaps, and conflicts in project execution, leading to inefficiencies and frustrations among team members.

Strategies for Improvement:

1. **Communication Protocols:** Establish clear communication protocols and channels for project communication, including regular meetings, email updates, and project management software.
2. **Role Clarity:** Define roles and responsibilities for each team member and stakeholder, clarifying expectations and accountabilities to ensure effective collaboration and coordination.
3. **Standardized Reporting:** Implement standardized reporting templates and timelines to ensure consistent and timely reporting of project progress, milestones, and issues.
4. **Stakeholder Engagement:** Foster stakeholder engagement and participation in project communication, soliciting feedback, and addressing concerns to promote transparency and accountability.
5. **Training and Development:** Provide training and development opportunities for project teams in communication skills, conflict resolution, and project management techniques to enhance communication effectiveness and teamwork.

Expected Outcomes: By implementing these strategies, ABC Corporation aims to achieve the following outcomes:

- Improved project communication and coordination
- Enhanced clarity and alignment on project requirements and expectations
- Timely and accurate reporting of project progress and issues
- Strengthened stakeholder relationships and engagement

Increased project efficiency and effectiveness

CHAPTER FIVE

ORAL COMMUNICATION AND MARKETING

Effective Meetings and Brainstorming Sessions:

- **Meeting Preparation:** Set clear objectives, develop an agenda, and invite relevant participants to ensure productive meetings.
- **Facilitation Techniques:** Use facilitation techniques such as active listening, summarizing key points, and managing time to keep meetings focused and on track.
- **Encouraging Participation:** Foster a collaborative environment where all participants feel comfortable sharing ideas and opinions during brainstorming sessions.

Voice Modulation, Intonation, and Pitch:

- **Voice Modulation:** Adjusting the tone, volume, and pace of speech to convey meaning and emotion effectively.
- **Intonation:** Using variations in pitch and stress patterns to emphasize key points and maintain listener engagement.
- **Pitch:** The perceived highness or lowness of a speaker's voice, which can influence how messages are received and interpreted.

Understanding Ads and Visual Semiotics:

- **Ads Analysis:** Analyze advertisements to understand their intended message, target audience, and persuasive techniques.
- **Visual Semiotics:** Interpret visual elements such as colors, symbols, and imagery to uncover underlying meanings and associations in advertisements.

Business Storytelling Techniques:

- **Narrative Structure:** Craft stories with a clear beginning, middle, and end to engage audiences and convey key messages effectively.
- **Emotional Appeal:** Use storytelling to evoke emotions and create connections with audiences, making messages more memorable and impactful.
- **Authenticity:** Share authentic and relatable stories that resonate with audiences and reinforce the organization's values and brand identity.

Creating and Delivering PPT Presentations:

- **Content Organization:** Structure presentations with a logical flow of information, using headings, bullet points, and visuals to enhance clarity and comprehension.
- **Visual Design:** Use professional and visually appealing slide designs, avoiding clutter and excessive text to maintain audience attention.
- **Delivery Techniques:** Practice effective delivery techniques such as eye contact, vocal projection, and body language to engage and captivate audiences during presentations.

Case Study: Enhancing Marketing Communication at XYZ Company

Background: XYZ Company, a software development firm, seeks to improve its marketing communication strategies to increase brand awareness and attract new clients. Despite offering innovative products, XYZ Company faces challenges in effectively communicating its value proposition and differentiators to target audiences.

Scenario: XYZ Company encounters the following marketing communication issues:

Ineffective Messaging: Marketing messages lack clarity and fail to effectively communicate the benefits and value of XYZ Company's products and services to potential clients.

Limited Reach: XYZ Company struggles to reach its target audience through traditional marketing channels, resulting in low visibility and brand recognition in the market.

Underutilized Visuals: Visual elements such as graphics, videos, and infographics are underutilized in marketing materials, missing opportunities to engage and captivate target audiences.

Inconsistent Branding: Inconsistent branding across different marketing channels and materials dilutes XYZ Company's brand identity and confuses potential clients about its offerings and positioning.

Strategies for Improvement:

1. **Message Refinement:** Refine marketing messages to clearly articulate XYZ Company's value proposition, unique selling points, and benefits to target audiences.
2. **Multi-channel Marketing:** Implement a multi-channel marketing strategy to reach target audiences through diverse platforms such as social media, email marketing, and content marketing.
3. **Visual Storytelling:** Leverage visual storytelling techniques to create compelling marketing materials that resonate with target audiences and convey key messages effectively.
4. **Brand Consistency:** Establish brand guidelines and ensure consistency in branding across all marketing materials and channels to strengthen brand identity and recognition.
5. **Analytics and Optimization:** Use analytics tools to track marketing performance, gather insights into audience engagement, and optimize marketing campaigns for better results.

Expected Outcomes: By implementing these strategies, XYZ Company aims to achieve the following outcomes:

- Increased brand awareness and visibility in the market
- Improved engagement and response rates from target audiences
- Enhanced brand identity and recognition through consistent branding
- Higher conversion rates and ROI from marketing efforts

CHAPTER SIX

CRISIS COMMUNICATION AND BRAND MANAGEMENT

Crisis Communication Strategies and Best Practices:

- **Preparation and Planning:** Develop a comprehensive crisis communication plan that includes protocols for identifying, assessing, and responding to potential crises.
- **Transparency and Timeliness:** Communicate openly and transparently with stakeholders, providing timely updates and accurate information to address concerns and mitigate rumors.
- **Stakeholder Engagement:** Engage with stakeholders, including employees, customers, media, and the public, to build trust, manage expectations, and demonstrate accountability during crises.
- **Consistency and Coordination:** Ensure consistency in messaging across all communication channels and coordinate efforts among internal and external stakeholders to maintain coherence and credibility.

Using Leadership Pitches for Crisis Management:

- **Leadership Presence:** Demonstrate strong leadership presence and authority in crisis situations, projecting confidence, empathy, and decisiveness to reassure stakeholders and inspire confidence.

- **Effective Communication:** Deliver clear, concise, and empathetic messages that acknowledge the severity of the situation, convey empathy for those affected, and outline the organization's response and commitment to resolution.
- **Media Engagement:** Proactively engage with the media to provide accurate information, address concerns, and shape the narrative surrounding the crisis, leveraging leadership pitches to convey key messages and manage perceptions effectively.

Managing Brand Image in Challenging Situations:

- **Brand Monitoring:** Monitor social media, news outlets, and other channels for mentions of the brand during crises, assessing sentiment and identifying emerging issues to inform strategic responses.
- **Reputation Management:** Implement reputation management strategies to protect and enhance the brand's image, including proactive communication, stakeholder engagement, and crisis preparedness.
- **Recovery and Resilience:** Demonstrate resilience and commitment to addressing the root causes of crises, rebuilding trust with stakeholders, and restoring the brand's reputation through transparent communication and tangible actions.

Case Study: Crisis Communication at XYZ Airlines

Background: XYZ Airlines, a leading airline company, faces a major crisis following a series of flight cancellations and delays due to unforeseen technical issues and adverse weather conditions. The crisis has resulted in widespread disruptions, passenger inconvenience, and negative media coverage, threatening the airline's reputation and brand image.

Scenario: XYZ Airlines encounters the following challenges in crisis communication and brand management:

Communication Breakdowns: Inadequate communication with passengers and stakeholders exacerbates confusion, frustration, and mistrust, leading to escalating tensions and public backlash.

Reputational Damage: Negative media coverage and social media chatter further tarnish XYZ Airlines' reputation, fueling public skepticism and criticism about the company's reliability and safety standards.

Leadership Response: The leadership team's response to the crisis lacks clarity, consistency, and empathy, further eroding confidence in the airline's ability to manage the situation effectively and prioritize passenger welfare.

Strategies for Improvement:

1. **Immediate Response:** Activate crisis communication protocols to provide timely updates, alternative travel arrangements, and compensation for affected passengers, demonstrating a commitment to passenger safety and satisfaction.
2. **Transparency and Accountability:** Communicate openly and transparently about the causes of the crisis, steps taken to address the issues, and measures implemented to prevent recurrence, fostering trust and credibility with passengers and stakeholders.
3. **Stakeholder Engagement:** Engage with passengers, employees, regulators, and the media to address concerns, answer questions, and solicit feedback, demonstrating a willingness to listen, learn, and improve based on stakeholder input.
4. **Reputation Recovery:** Implement a comprehensive reputation recovery plan that includes proactive communication, service recovery initiatives, and long-term improvements to operational resilience and customer experience.
5. **Continuous Improvement:** Conduct post-crisis reviews and evaluations to identify lessons learned, areas for improvement, and opportunities to strengthen crisis preparedness and response capabilities for future incidents.

Expected Outcomes: By implementing these strategies, XYZ Airlines aims to achieve the following outcomes:

- Restored trust and confidence in the airline's reliability, safety, and customer service standards.
- Enhanced reputation and brand resilience through transparent communication and effective crisis management.
- Strengthened relationships with passengers, stakeholders, and the public, fostering long-term loyalty and advocacy for the airline.
- Improved operational resilience and crisis preparedness to mitigate the impact of future incidents and disruptions.

CHAPTER SEVEN

Overcoming Communication Barriers

Understanding Communication Barriers:

Communication barriers are obstacles that prevent effective exchange of information, ideas, and messages within an organization. These barriers can arise due to various factors such as language differences, cultural norms, technological limitations, and psychological barriers. Understanding these barriers is essential for identifying and addressing communication challenges within the workplace.

Strategies for Overcoming Barriers:

Several strategies can be employed to overcome communication barriers:

1. **Clear and Concise Messaging:** Ensuring that messages are clear, concise, and easy to understand can help minimize misunderstandings and misinterpretations.
2. **Active Listening:** Encouraging active listening among team members fosters better understanding and promotes empathy and rapport.
3. **Feedback Mechanisms:** Implementing feedback mechanisms allows for the exchange of constructive criticism and suggestions for improvement, improving communication effectiveness.
4. **Cultural Sensitivity Training:** Providing training on cultural differences and norms helps employees navigate diverse workplace environments and promotes inclusivity.

5. **Technological Solutions:** Leveraging technology such as video conferencing, collaboration tools, and communication platforms facilitates virtual communication and reduces technological barriers.

Effective Communication Strategies:
Effective communication strategies enhance organizational communication and promote a positive work environment:

1. **Open Communication:** Encouraging open dialogue and transparency fosters trust and collaboration among team members.
2. **Adaptability:** Being adaptable to different communication styles and preferences accommodates diverse workforce needs and enhances communication effectiveness.
3. **Clarity and Consistency:** Maintaining clarity and consistency in communication ensures that messages are understood accurately and reduces the likelihood of confusion.
4. **Empathy:** Practicing empathy and understanding others' perspectives promotes effective interpersonal communication and conflict resolution.
5. **Leadership Communication:** Effective leadership communication sets clear expectations, provides guidance, and fosters a shared vision among team members.

Organizational Communication Models:
Organizational communication models provide frameworks for understanding communication processes within organizations:

1. **Linear Model:** The linear model depicts communication as a one-way process, with a sender transmitting a message through a channel to a receiver. Feedback may be provided, but the process is linear and sequential.
2. **Transactional Model:** The transactional model views communication as a dynamic process involving simultaneous encoding and decoding of messages by both sender and receiver. Feedback is continuous, and communication is influenced by context and feedback.

Critical Organizational Communication:
Critical organizational communication examines power dynamics, social inequalities, and cultural hegemony within organizational structures. It

challenges traditional approaches to communication by highlighting issues of social justice, equity, and inclusivity.

Case Study: Overcoming Communication Challenges in a Multinational Corporation

Background:

Smith & Sons Enterprises is a family-owned construction company that has been operating for over three decades. The company specializes in residential and commercial construction projects in the local area. Despite its long-standing presence in the industry, Smith & Sons Enterprises is facing communication challenges that are impacting its efficiency and profitability.

Scenario:

Smith & Sons Enterprises is experiencing communication breakdowns at various levels within the organization:

Interdepartmental Communication: Communication between different departments, such as project management, procurement, and operations, is inefficient and often leads to delays in project timelines. Lack of coordination and collaboration between teams hinders project progress and affects overall productivity.

Generational Communication Divide: The company's workforce consists of employees from different generations, including Baby Boomers, Generation X, and Millennials. The generational gap leads to communication barriers, misunderstandings, and resistance to change. Traditional communication methods favored by older employees may not resonate with younger generations, leading to conflicts and inefficiencies.

Family Dynamics: As a family-owned business, interpersonal relationships among family members impact communication within the company. Disagreements, conflicts, and power struggles among family members spill over into business operations, affecting decision-making processes and organizational culture.

Client Communication: Communication with clients, subcontractors, and suppliers is often inconsistent and lacks clarity. Miscommunication regarding project specifications, timelines, and expectations results in client dissatisfaction and project delays.

Strategies for Improvement:

1. **Establish Clear Communication Channels:** Implement structured communication channels within the organization to ensure that

information flows smoothly between departments. Regular meetings, project updates, and communication protocols can help streamline interdepartmental communication.

2. **Training and Development:** Provide communication training and professional development opportunities for employees to enhance their communication skills. Offer workshops on active listening, conflict resolution, and effective communication strategies tailored to different generational preferences.

3. **Implement Technology Solutions:** Invest in communication tools and software that facilitate collaboration and information sharing. Project management platforms, cloud-based document storage, and communication apps can improve efficiency and transparency in communication processes.

4. **Family Business Governance:** Establish clear governance structures and decision-making processes for family-owned businesses. Implementing formal policies and procedures for conflict resolution and succession planning can mitigate family-related communication challenges and foster a harmonious work environment.

5. **Client Relationship Management:** Improve client communication by setting clear expectations, providing regular project updates, and soliciting feedback. Enhance transparency and accountability in client interactions to build trust and strengthen long-term relationships.

Expected Outcomes:

By implementing these strategies, Smith & Sons Enterprises aims to achieve the following outcomes:

- Improved interdepartmental coordination and collaboration
- Enhanced communication effectiveness across generational divides
- Strengthened family relationships and governance structures
- Increased client satisfaction and retention
- Greater efficiency and profitability in business operations

Conclusion:

Effective communication is essential for the success of any organization, especially in family-owned businesses where interpersonal relationships play a significant role. By addressing communication challenges proactively and implementing strategies to improve communication at various levels,

Smith & Sons Enterprises can overcome obstacles and achieve its business objectives in a competitive market environment.

9 7 9 8 8 9 4 9 8 0 0 0 3